Count Your Way through
Russia

by Jim Haskins

illustrations by Vera Mednikov

Carolrhoda Books, Inc./Minneapolis

To Elisa Beth and the future

Text copyright © 1987 by Jim Haskins
Illustrations copyright © 1987 by Carolrhoda Books, Inc.

This book is available in two editions:
Library binding by Carolrhoda Books, Inc.
Soft cover by First Avenue Editions
241 First Avenue North
Minneapolis, Minnesota 55401

LIBRARY OF CONGRESS CATALOGING-IN-PUBLICATION DATA

Haskins, James, 1941-
  Count your way through Russia.

  Summary: Presents the numbers one through ten in
Russian, using each number to introduce concepts about
the Soviet Union and Russian culture.
  1. Soviet Union—Juvenile literature. 2. Counting—
Juvenile literature. [1. Soviet Union. 2. Counting]
I. Mednikov, Vera, ill. II. Title.
DK43.H39 1987   947   87-6397
  ISBN 0-87614-303-6 (lib bdg.)
  ISBN 0-87614-488-1 (pbk.)

Manufactured in the United States of America

  3   4   5   6   7   8   9   10   97   96   95   94   93   92   91   90   89

Introductory Note

The Russian language, like the English language, has one alphabet. This alphabet, called the Cyrillic alphabet, has 33 letters, which are used to form all Russian words. The Russian language uses Arabic numerals to make up their number system as do many other languages, including English.

While counting your way through Russia, you will find three different names for this huge country. Officially named the Union of Soviet Socialist Republics (USSR), this country is more often referred to as the Soviet Union or as Russia. Russia is actually the name of the largest of the 15 republics that make up the USSR, but many people call the whole country Russia when they speak of its culture or way of life.

ОДИН ○ **1** ○ (ah-DEEN)

There is only **one** Kremlin, and it is the most famous group of buildings in the USSR. Located in Moscow, it is the center of government for the Soviet Union. The Kremlin began as a wooden fortress in 1156, and what stands today is the result of centuries of continual construction and rebuilding. The 66-acre enclosed area includes magnificent cathedrals, monasteries, palaces, a theater, a museum, and a modern office building. Many of Russia's most valuable artistic and historical treasures are kept in the Kremlin.

ДВА ● **2** ● (dvah)

Two snowshoes are needed for walking outside during the long winters of the northwestern, central, and eastern parts of the Soviet Union. These areas have snow and ice for many months of the year. Around the White Sea, winter lasts for about nine months, and far northern Siberia has ice and snow for ten months of each year. The Soviet Union is so big, however, that there are also places that are very hot for most of the year.

ТРИ  **3** (tree)

Troika (TROY-kuh) is a Russian word meaning a group of **three**. A Russian sleigh drawn by three horses that are side by side is called a *troika*, and in the Soviet Union a three-part form of government is also known as a *troika*.

ЧЕТЫРЕ ○ 4 ○ (chih-TEE-reh)

The Soviet Union has more land area than any other country in the world. It takes **four** days to go just halfway across the Soviet Union on the Trans-Siberian Express train.

ПЯТЬ 5 (pyaht)

It takes **five** people to dance the *Pereplyas* (pare-uh-plee-us), a popular folk dance in Russia. The name *Pereplyas* means to dance longer and better than others. The five people try to outdo each other in skill and in making up new steps.

The dancers wear their national costume, which usually consists of an embroidered shirt and trousers that are tucked into black boots.

ШЕСТЬ ● **6** ● (shayst)

Six times in a row, from 1964 to 1984, Russian couples won the Olympic gold medal for pairs figure skating. These athletes spent long hours training to be the best in their sport.

СЕМЬ  **(seeaym)**

The number **seven** is very important in Russian culture. There are seven domes on churches and seven bells in bell towers. One of the most popular items of Russian folk art is the set of seven nesting dolls called *Matryoshka* (mah-tree-OSH-kuh). Each doll fits inside the next until they are all inside of the seventh and largest doll.

ВОСЕМЬ 8 (VOH-seeaym)

For Russian women, the number **eight** is especially important. On March 8 each year, the Soviet Union celebrates Women's Day. Schools and offices are closed for the day, and many women receive flowers from their family. It is official policy in the Soviet Union that women and men have the same rights.

ДЕВЯТЬ ● 9 ● (DYEH-veht)

While there are many places to live in the Soviet Union, more and more Russians are moving to the cities. Because of housing shortages in many cities, new apartment buildings are being built. In order to house large numbers of people, most are at least **nine** stories tall.

ДЕСЯТЬ ● 10 ● (DYEH-seht)

At the age of **ten**, Russian boys and girls may join the Young Pioneers, a youth organization that offers recreational activities and encourages patriotism. They attend meetings at Young Pioneer "palaces," which are not really palaces but places to take part in hobbies and the arts. In the summer, members may go to Young Pioneer camps.

Pronunciation Guide

1 / **ОДИН** / ah-DEEN
2 / **ДВА** / dvah
3 / **ТРИ** / tree
4 / **ЧЕТЫРЕ** / chih-TEE-reh
5 / **ПЯТЬ** / pyaht
6 / **ШЕСТЬ** / shayst
7 / **СЕМЬ** / seeaym
8 / **ВОСЕМЬ** / VOH-seeaym
9 / **ДЕВЯТЬ** / DYEH-veht
10 / **ДЕСЯТЬ** / DYEH-seht